The Throws and Take-downs of

Sombo
Russian
Wrestling

Geoff Thompson

SUMMERSDALE

Summersdale Publishers Ltd
46 West Street
Chichester
West Sussex
PO19 1RP
United Kingdom

www.summersdale.com

Printed and bound in Great Britain.

ISBN 1 84024 027 X

First edit by Kerry Thompson.

Photographs by David W. Monks, member of the Master Photographers' Association
Snappy Snaps Portrait Studio
7 Cross Cheaping
Coventry
CV1 1HF

About the author

Geoff Thompson has written over 20 books and is known worldwide for his bestselling autobiography, *Watch My Back*, about his nine years working as a nightclub doorman. He currently has a quarter of a million books in print. He holds the rank of 6th Dan black belt in Japanese karate, 1st Dan in judo and is also qualified to senior instructor level in various other forms of wrestling and martial arts. He has several scripts for stage and screen in development with Destiny Films.

He has published articles for *GQ* magazine, and has also been featured in *FHM*, *Maxim*, *Arena*, *Front* and *Loaded* magazines, and has appeared many times on mainstream television.
Geoff is currently a contributing editor for *Men's Fitness* magazine.

Geoff qualified as a sombo instructor after training privately under the Master of Sport, former Moscow sombo club champion Vadim Kolganov. He is a recognised sombo instructor with Mathew Clempner's FORMA (Federation of Russian Martial Arts).

For a free colour brochure of Geoff Thompson's
books and videos please ring the
24-hour hotline on 02476 431100 or write to:

Geoff Thompson Ltd
PO Box 307
Coventry
CV3 2YP

www.geoffthompson.com

www.summersdale.com

Contents

The History of Sombo by Vadim Kolganov

Whilst there are many systems around under the guise of Russian wrestling, sombo is the authentic Russian art in its pure form and not a derivative.

Since ancient times man has developed different types of physical exercise which were used in combat training. The most popular exercise was grappling or wrestling in one form or another. In the folklore of most nations there was an ideal hero who had extraordinary, even magical, physical and spiritual powers which enabled him to fight evil forces. One of the main characteristics of these heroes – Gilgamesh in Babylon, Ozikis in Egypt, Hercules in Greece, great U in China, Igreid in Germany, Ruslem in Tibet, Illya Murometz in Russia – was that they were all unbeatable masters of wrestling.

Sombo Russian Wrestling

In Egypt physical exercise, especially wrestling, has existed for a long time; evidence of this has been found in the pyramids of the Pharaohs and nobles. In one pyramid about 400 pictures were discovered that depicted different wrestling techniques, recognisable even today.

The ancient Greeks also played an important role in the history of physical culture. They developed a strong system of physical training as early as the ninth century BC that is still useful today. In schools (*Palestas*) specialist teachers developed programmes to train young athletes in wrestling, sprinting, long jump, juggling and discus throwing. This formed the basis of what later became known as the Pentathlon.

The first rules of competition for wrestling were laid down by Tazaem, the founder of Athens.

The Olympic games were begun in Ancient Greece (776 BC) and wrestling was in the first programme both as an independent sport and also as a component part of pancratium – a combination of fist fighting and wrestling (circa 648 BC).

Rome also played an essential part in the development of wrestling. The Romans didn't follow the Greek philosophy of all-round athletic development; they leaned more toward military type training. During the upsurge of feudalism in Europe (eleventh to fifteenth century AD) a system of training for knights was also developed that included fighting contests with and without weapons.

Talhoffer's fifteenth-century book of wrestling was one of the first texts on the subjects and the illustrations in the book show self-defence techniques that are very similar to modern ju-jitsu.

Medieval manuscripts and calendars show that wrestling featured very heavily in celebrations of the day such as fairs and weddings. During this time most countries were developing systems of physical exercise which clearly

Sombo Russian Wrestling

expressed their national character, but in spite of the different principles and aims of these countries, they all included fencing, running, swimming and wrestling.

Wrestling in Russia was developed from techniques taken from many countries. Strength, adroitness and endurance were long-admired fighting characteristics and thus festive gatherings always ended in a wrestling contest. Wrestling was often seen as a way of solving arguments in Russian towns: there was even a special place built to stage these matches. Sombo wrestling was born in Russia as a result of exhaustive research by Soviet coaches and sportsmen.

In sport-sombo, all national and international wrestling techniques can be used and combat-sombo also incorporates the best elements from different systems of self-defence. Because of this rich and varied technical arsenal, sombo is often referred to as 'the invisible weapon' – the weapon that is always with you.

The History of Sombo by Vadim Kolganov

Sombo wrestling is one of the youngest sports in Russia but it would be difficult to find another sport with a more interesting or complex history. Sombo came not from one but from several different and diverse sources. Even the name itself was repeatedly changed as the art developed: 'self-defence', 'samoz', 'system sam', 'freestyle wrestling', 'freestyle sombo wrestling', and then finally 'sombo wrestling'. There are no definite dates for the birth of this great art. Some believe it began in November 1938, the year it was officially recognised as a cultivated sport within the Soviet Union. Others say that sombo wrestling contests were taking place earlier in the 1930s. Another school of thought believes that a prototype of sombo was taking shape in the early 1920s. Traditionally it is considered that sombo was invented by three outstanding men; V. A. Spiridonov, B. C. Oshepkov and A. A. Xarlampiev. Each of these Masters of Sport played a pivotal role in the conception of sombo.

Sombo wrestling is all about the will to win, fitness, courage, strength, quickness and adroitness. Training in sombo helps sportsmen to defend themselves without resorting to weaponry. Thus, it is an excellent sport or art for anybody in the field of self-defence and one with which I am proud to be affiliated.

I am sure that this book by my student Geoff Thompson will help you to these ends.

Vadim Kolganov – Russian coach of sombo wrestling and Master of Sport at the Central Academy of Sport, Moscow 1986 – 1991

Introduction

Before I start, I would like to explain that this is not meant to be a comprehensive book on sombo wrestling throws and take-downs, neither am I aiming to represent anyone else other than myself. The techniques in this book are my own personal favourites from the sombo system – nothing more, nothing less.

There has been a lot said of late about the art of grappling, especially the ground fighting aspects of the art. The grappling arts seem to be enjoying a well-earned and long-awaited revival.

Grappling was in vogue in the early part of this century, or the Golden Age of Wrestling as it was known, but its popularity died off just before – and partly due to – the First World War. After the war it enjoyed something of a revival but more in the form of show wrestling.

Sombo Russian Wrestling

More recently grappling seems to have been hidden within the shadow of contemporary combat; this is probably due to its candid demeanour. Its devastating potency is cloaked by a dishevelled front; people were – and still are – naturally drawn towards the superfluously spectacular kicking arts that have been the popular flavour for quite some time now.

However, the world of combat has at last evolved and many of the more spectacular arts have failed the acid test of time, not to mention the pressures of reality. The 'prettier' systems that originally had thousands flocking to dojos around the world have fallen at the obstacle of practicality proving to be less effective than their PR would suggest. The fundamental movements of the grappling arts, so often ignored due to the 'ugly duckling' syndrome, have risen to the surface and the swan of real combat has blossomed.

A lot of what happens in floor fighting (unless you are an exceptional player) is wholly determined by how you got there in the first place. If you are thrown to the floor and end in a bad position you may never escape from there, or your opponent may be in a position to stand back up and kick pieces off you while you are on your back. In the controlled arena we tend to practise ground fighting from a neutral position where both fighters have an equal start. In a real situation there is no such luxury and you very much have to make the best of what you are given – unless of course you're the one who controls the take-down – which is what this book is all about.

The question that I'm most often asked in relation to ground fighting is, 'How do you get to that position from vertical fighting?'

Hopefully in this series of books on throws and take-downs I will be able to answer that question sensibly, if not comprehensively.

In this volume we will be looking at the throws and take-downs of sombo. Having studied this system with an authentic

Sombo Russian Wrestling

Russian Master of Sport, former Moscow club champion Vadim Kolganov, I can vouch for the potency and dynamism of this young and, as yet, little heard of art.

As with ground fighting don't make the throws and take-downs the be all and end all of your fighting arsenal, many opponents in a live scenario will not allow you to throw them cleanly, they will grip you as though their very lives depend upon it and drag you to the floor with them, if you don't know how to fight on the floor then you might be in trouble.

Use this book in combination with a good class (or partner); there is nothing like a real opponent to perfect the physical technique, I'd go as far as to say that it cannot be learned properly by book alone. Learn the fundamentals of the technique, and then put it under the pressure of a non-compliant partner. Once you can successfully use the technique against someone that doesn't want to be thrown, then you know you have the technique.

Compliance in training kills; it's only of use when first learning the fundamentals of a technique, once learned an opponent should offer 100 per cent resistance and also try to throw you. Taking the randori (free-fighting or sparring) out of a system is effectively taking the teeth out of it.

Best of luck to you with the practise and thank you for taking the time to read this book.

Chapter One
Balance, Stance, Grip

The fundamentals of balance are pretty much the same with all the grappling arts, so if you have read the other books in this series, forgive me for repeating myself.

Lets start at the beginning (it's a very good place to start). Knowing all the throws in the world won't help if you haven't got the balance and stance right. It is hard to throw an opponent and easy to be thrown when the balance is off. To be honest, balance is best developed when actually fighting on the mat with another player. What I'd like to give you here are the basics so that you can practise it correctly from the very beginning. I know when I first started in the grappling arts I made the mistake of practising without supervision and ended up being very good at doing techniques the wrong way. Getting the basics right is essential. So take your time with it and try not to rush ahead. Like any job worth doing, preparation is all. Hopefully what this book will do is act as an appetiser for you to actually start a sombo class or, like me, perhaps take private lessons from an expert. Mathew Clempner runs an excellent class for Russian martial arts and I highly recommend him. His advert is at the back of this book.

We will start by working from a left lead stance; this can be changed if you prefer to lead with your right side, just reverse the instructions as I lay them out. Presuming that you are working from a left lead stance you should stand in a small 45-degree stance.

Sombo Russian Wrestling

Bend slightly at the knees and relax. The 45-degree is where you find your balance to throw and to prevent yourself from being thrown. Try to maintain this stance at all times. The only time you should change is when you enter to take a throw. Whether the throw is successful or not you should immediately revert back to the stance, if you do successfully throw the opponent you can follow him down to ground fighting or stay vertical and finish him from there (or run away if the altercation is in the street).

Grip the opponent's right lapel (or shirt, coat, neck, hair) with your left hand and his left sleeve or wrist or, in the case of wrestling, perhaps around the back of the triceps (upper arm) with your right. This is the basic stance and grip to take when looking for a throw. In the street you might not be able to choose your grip, in this case you may have to make do with what is given. It matters not because once the throws have been practised you should be able to take an opponent over from any grip and from any position. For now we will work with the fundamentals. Later you can look at more advanced methodologies. The grips being described in this book are nothing more than basic but, depending upon how serious you are about the practice of sombo, a whole plethora of different grips can be developed. At high-level competitions it is usually the better grip fighter that dominates and wins the fight. For now, basic grips are fine; you are unlikely to be meeting any trained grapplers in a street attack.

Once you have the basic stance and grip you can use it to break the opponent's balance. On a mat you will be working with players who generally trained well in defending their balance and it becomes a game of breaking balance as a precursor to the throw. In fact with a player of equal skill you are very unlikely to throw them at all without breaking balance first.

You can break the opponent's balance in a number of ways; with pulling or pushing actions, or by attempting or feigning one throw to leave him open and vulnerable for another. You break the opponent's balance by pushing or pulling him to the left rear, directly behind, to the right rear or directly to his right or left. Alternatively you can pull the opponent directly towards you, to your left or right rear or directly to the right or left. You can also pull him downward.

Any one of these actions will force the opponent to move, hopefully out of stance and off balance, and when he does you can execute a throw.

The other time to take an opponent off balance and take the throw is when he makes an attack (a throw or punch) and you take advantage of his stance change to take him over. All throwing actions rely heavily on feeling their energy and using it. This is something that has to be felt and cannot be properly related via the pages of a book.

Stiff Arming

This is a problem in most forms of grappling.

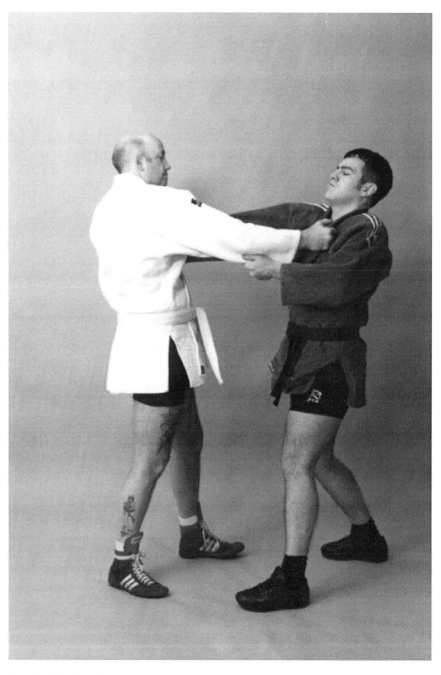

It usually occurs with less skilful opponents, especially the type that you will meet in a street encounter, who literally hold you to the spot with their strength, normally out of sheer terror. They don't attack or defend, they just hold on for dear life and once they grip it can be very difficult to get them off. I had a chap grip me with a stiff arm outside a Coventry nightclub; he held so tightly that even when I butted him unconscious and he fell to the floor, he was still holding on to my shirt and pulled it right off my back. Dealing with stiff armers requires good grip work and a good sense of flow; use their strength against them by going with the flow of energy. If it's a street encounter, kick them in the bollocks or butt them in the face before you attempt a throw, in fact, just strike them with any available technique first. It goes without saying that in most sport-grappling this would be an illegal move (I should know, I have tried more than once), so don't do it. Well, you can if you want to but don't say that I said you could! The blow before the throw will break the balance of even the strongest stiff armer and thus create a window of opportunity for you to bang in the throw.

Sombo Russian Wrestling

If you encounter a fighter with no substantial clothing to grab then the throwing technique has to change slightly. This has happened to me many times when facing people with thin T-shirts or even people who pull their tops off as part of their ritualistic posturing. It can be murderous trying to get a grip on a slippery torso (but enough about my sex life). In these circumstances you need to revert to the wrestling-type throws and use the opponent's limbs, as opposed to the apparel, to throw. From my experience of working with several systems of grappling, the wrestling take-downs are the favourites here because they don't rely on clothing to make a throw happen. Some of the Greco (Greco-Roman wrestling) snatches and freestyle leg take-downs come into their own in this scenario.

Having said that, give me a guy in heavy tweed and I'll make any throw happen. Again, this is not to say that you can't use judo or sombo if the opponent hasn't got a jacket on; you can, you may just have to adjust the technique slightly.

It is important that you have a good pull around with an opponent (preferably lots of different opponents) to get used to balance, grip and entries for the throws: the more times you are on the mat (but not on your back) the better.

Chapter Two
Double Leg Pick-up

The double leg pick-up is a lovely take-down and is usually taken from outside gripping range – that is, you take the throw before you take a grip on the opponent. Very often the attacker will employ this take-down at the same time his opponent strikes to take a grip on him, using the element of surprise as an entry. It can also be used if you have fallen, or been knocked to the floor and are on your knees in front an opponent.

It has been called the 'rugger' style attack because it resembles the type of tackle that a rugby player would use. It is a very instinctive throw and when used properly it can be devastating. The sombo players like this particular throw because it leaves the thrower still holding the opponent's legs, ideal for finishing with one of the many leg locks that the Russian players love to employ.

Double Leg Pick-up

We will work the attack from just outside of gripping range. Lunge forward under the opponent's arms and grab around the back of his legs. Your head should go to the opponent's right side. Bend deeply at the knees and pick the opponent off the floor. Keep your back as straight as you can; the strength of the pick-up should come from your legs. Slam his back or head into the floor.

Be careful when using this technique that you don't get your head caught in the guillotine choke on the way in.

From here you have the choice to take the play to the floor, leg lock from where you are, or let go and finish with your feet.

Sombo Russian Wrestling

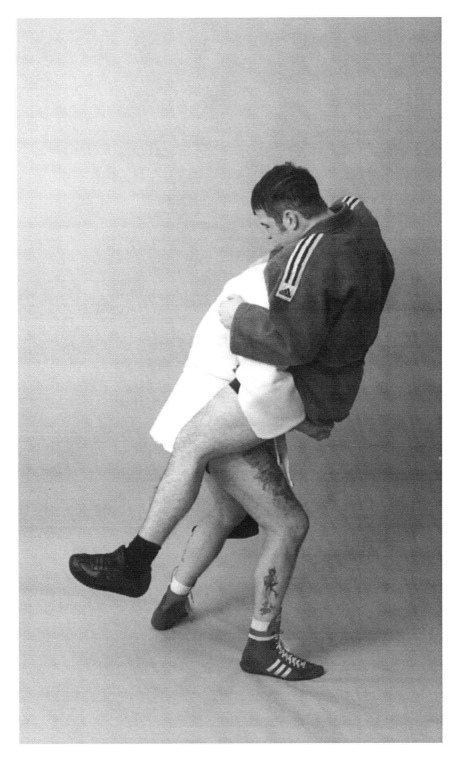

Sombo Russian Wrestling

If you find yourself already on your knees on the floor and in front of an opponent (this generally happens if you get caught off guard and have been struck by an opponent), wrap your arms around the backs of his legs and tuck your head into the side of his thigh, drive forward with your legs and take the opponent to the floor.

Double Leg Pick-up

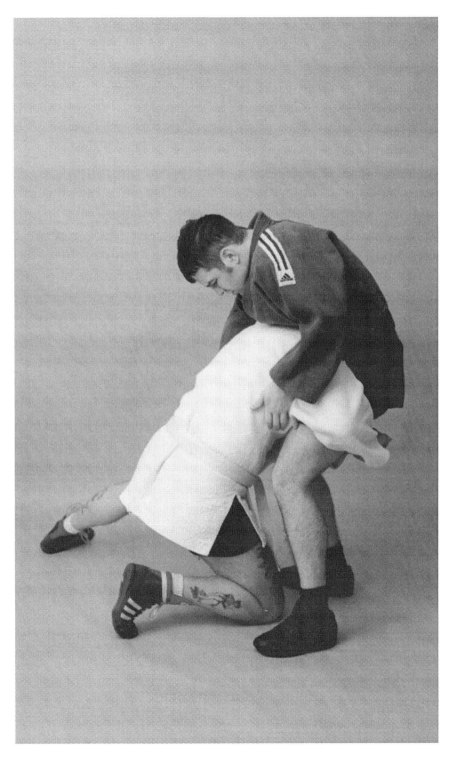

Sombo Russian Wrestling

Double Leg Pick-up

A word of warning here: because this take-down is taken from outside of gripping range it might imply that I think you should use this instead of the more immediate punching range. For the record I believe that no throw should be taken when the option of punching is still open to you. The punching range is the main artillery range for close combat. Throws and take-downs, in my opinion, should only be used as support. There are exceptions but the general rule of thumb is never go to the grappling range unless you absolutely have to.

Chapter Three
Single Leg to Double Leg Take-down

The single leg to double leg take-down is very similar to the double leg take-down, only this time we are working from a grip.

The reason I particularly like this technique is because it works brilliantly from catching a leg that the opponent has tried to attack you with. Very often in a real encounter an opponent tries to kick or knee you and you catch his leg and then don't know what to do with it. The trick is to take advantage of the caught leg and throw the opponent over by using it as an appendage.

This works equally well if you catch a foot, a knee or if you simply bend down and pick the opponent's leg off the floor. For the sake of example we will work from simply picking the leg off the floor.

Single Leg to Double Leg Take-down

Working from a right grip with a right lead stance, release your left hand from the grip on the opponent's sleeve, reach down and wrap your left arm around the back of his knee, picking his right leg off the floor. From here you are in a position to take an assortment of throws and take-downs. The one you choose is usually determined by what the opponent offers you.

Release your right grip on the opponent's lapel, bend down, using your legs more than your back, and hook your right arm around the back of the opponent's left leg. Pick him off the floor and slam him down.

Sombo Russian Wrestling

Single Leg to Double Leg Take-down

Sombo Russian Wrestling

Chapter Four
Single Leg Pick-up, Reverse Leg Inner Reap

This is a variation of the leg pick-up or the leg catch and it is a variation that I love to employ because it is so easily available. Working from a right grip with a right lead stance, release your left hand from the grip on the opponent's sleeve, reach down and wrap your left arm around the back of his knee, picking his right leg off the floor. Keep your right grip on the lapel, hook your right leg around the back (inside) of the opponent's left supporting leg and reap it off the floor, simultaneously driving him backwards with your right grip and slamming him on to his back or head.

This is a very malleable technique in that, once reaped off the floor, the thrower has the control and the potential to be able to land the opponent on the back of his head in a debilitating action or gently ease him to the floor – depending upon the severity of the situation.

Sombo Russian Wrestling

Single Leg Pick-up, Reverse Leg Inner Reap

Sombo Russian Wrestling

If the guy is trying to take your life you may feel that he needs taking to unconsciousness; if he is just a mouth and you feel that the threat is not so great then you have the power to be a little gentler.

This same technique can be employed in exactly the same way, but without the reap, by placing (as opposed to reaping and lifting) your right leg behind the opponent's left leg and just pushing him over it in a tripping action.

Single Leg Pick-up, Reverse Leg Inner Reap

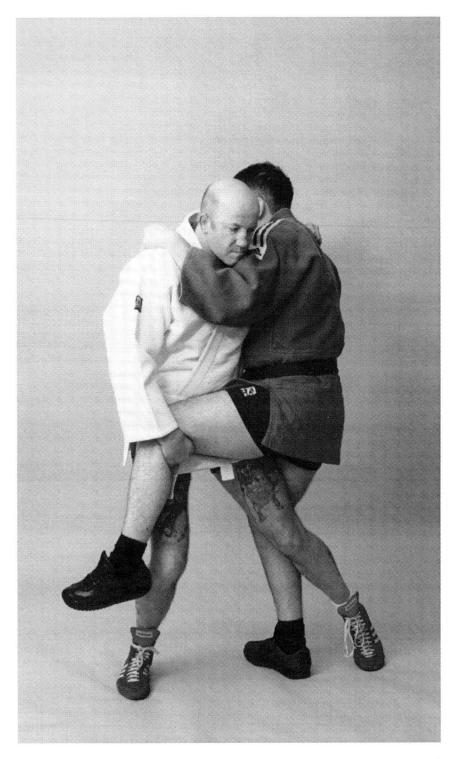

Chapter Five
Single Leg Pick-up, Reverse Leg Outer Reap

This is virtually the same as the last technique, only we are reaping the reverse, with the support leg on the outside as opposed to the inside. This is a more technical throw to employ but the injury potential to the opponent is greater because of the awkward and high fall from the throw.

Working from a right grip and a right lead stance, release your left hand from the grip on the opponent's sleeve, reach down and wrap your left arm around the back of his knee, picking his right leg off the floor. Keep your right grip on the lapel, hook your left leg around the back and outside, of the opponent's left supporting leg and reap it off the floor, simultaneously driving him backwards with your right grip and slamming him on to his back or head.

Single leg Pick-up, Reverse Leg Outer Reap

Sombo Russian Wrestling

Single leg Pick-up, Reverse Leg Outer Reap

Sombo Russian Wrestling

This also is a very malleable technique and how you employ it depends upon the severity of the situation.

This same technique can be employed in exactly the same way, but without the reap, by placing (as opposed to reaping and lifting) your left leg behind the opponent's left leg and just pushing him over it in a tripping action.

Single leg Pick-up, Reverse Leg Outer Reap

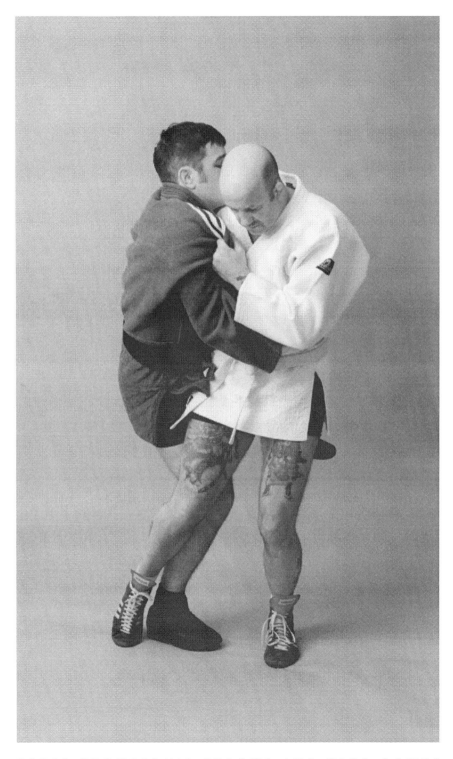

Chapter Six
Single Leg Pick-up, Minor Inner Reap

Taking the single leg take-down with a minor reap, or trip, is another excellent way of taking an opponent off his feet. Personally I like to use the minor reap in a kicking or sweeping action, literally kicking the opponent off the support leg without worry of injuring their ankle en route. Outside the chippy this would be ideal but in the controlled arena you do have to take a little more care not to injure your partner.

Working from a right grip and a right lead stance, release your left hand from the grip on the opponent's sleeve, reach down and wrap your left arm around the back of his knee, picking his right leg off the floor. Keep your right grip on the lapel, hook your left leg around the back and outside of the opponent's left supporting ankle and reap or sweep it off the floor, simultaneously driving him backwards with your left grip and slamming him on to his back or head.

Single Leg Pick-up, Minor Inner Reap

Sombo Russian Wrestling

Single Leg Pick-up, Minor Inner Reap

Again, this same technique can be employed in exactly the same way, but without the reap, by placing (as opposed to reaping and lifting) your left leg behind the opponent's left leg and just pushing him over it in a tripping action.

Sombo Russian Wrestling

Chapter Seven
Single Leg Pick-up, Body Drop

Adding the body drop to the single leg pick-up takes the throw to another dimension. Very few people, especially in the street scenario, ever get back up from this take-down. However, it is a more complicated throw to master. The results though are worth the extra training time on the mat.

Working from a right grip with a right lead stance, release your right hand from the grip on the opponent's sleeve, reach down and wrap your right arm around the back of his left knee, picking his leg off the floor. Turn your back into the opponent and bring your left leg behind you in a semi-circular action. Then thrust your right leg across in front of the opponent's supporting leg and simultaneously push his left leg high to take his balance and pull down hard on his left sleeve so that he trips over your right leg. Make sure that you bend your left leg at the knee and thrust it straight as you pull him over your right leg. Slam him hard into the floor.

Sombo Russian Wrestling

Single Leg Pick-up, Body Drop

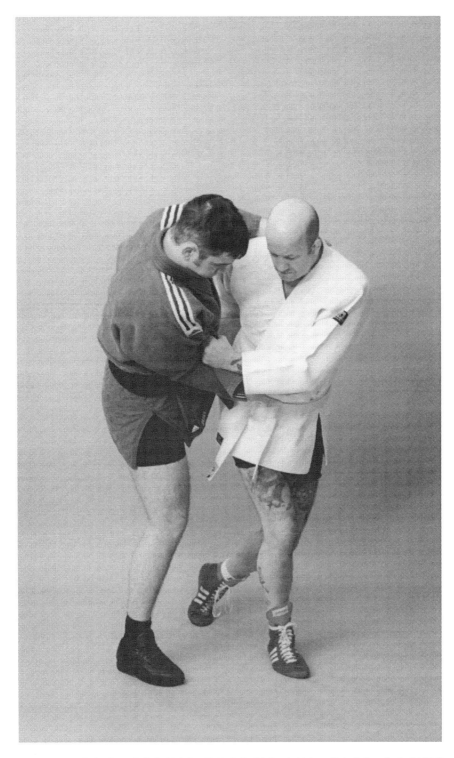

Sombo Russian Wrestling

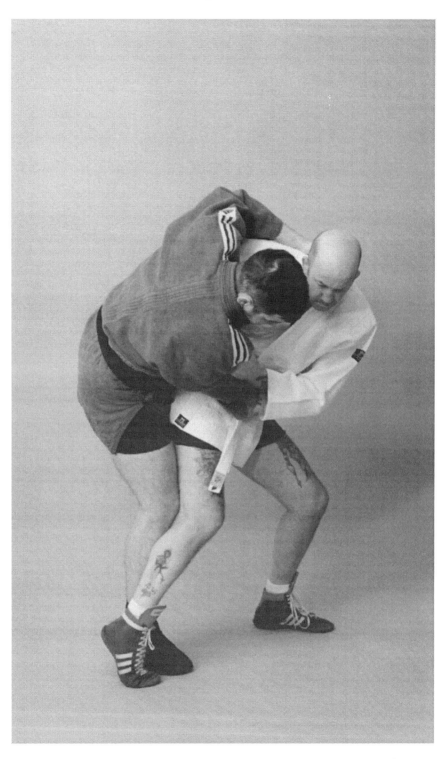

Chapter Eight
Ankle Pick-up

Often it's the simplest throws that work the best when the proverbial poo hits the fan. The ankle pick-up falls into this category because it is so simple, and yet so effective in taking a fellow to the floor. I find that these work well from the standard grip, but they also work very well if you are prostrate and your opponent is vertical.

Just recently one of my own students made the mistake of going to the floor with an attacker outside a busy nightclub. He was controlling him well when, as is often the case in the street scenario, one of his opponent's friends ran over and tried to attack my student whilst he was on still on the ground. My student grabbed around the back of the vertical opponent's ankle, pushed his elbow into his calf and drove him over with only one hand. So this technique, once learned, has many possible adaptations that can be employed on and off the mat.

Sombo Russian Wrestling

From a right lapel grip, reach down and grab around the back of the opponent's right ankle with your left hand. Pull his foot off the floor and towards you whilst simultaneously pulling his weight, with your right hand, over to your left.

Sombo Russian Wrestling

Chapter Nine
Ankle Pick-up (Inside)

With the inside ankle pick-up we employ the elbow into the opponent's calf to drive him over. It is a simple but effective technique that takes many opponents by surprise.

From a left hand lapel grip, reach down and grab around the back of the opponent's ankle from the inside, thrusting your elbow into the inside of his calf muscle. Simultaneously pull at the ankle and push with the elbow to drive the opponent over.

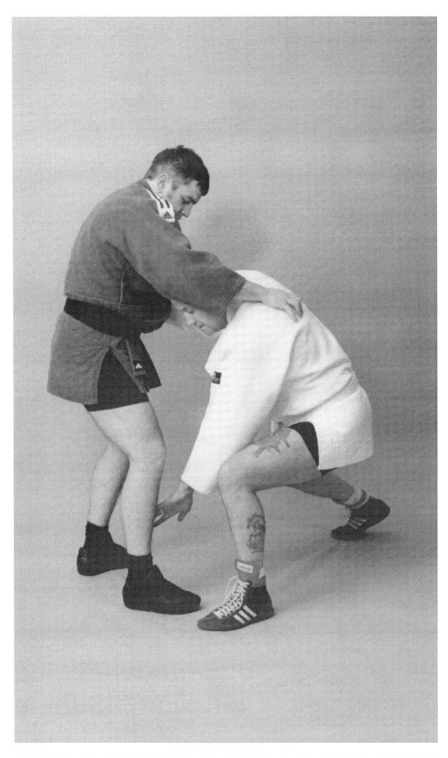

Sombo Russian Wrestling

Chapter Ten
Belt-assisted Hip Throw

The Russian players love using the opponent's belt to aid in certain throws. You might say that this is unrealistic because, in the street, attackers are very unlikely to be wearing a martial arts belt, and you'd be right. What I have found though is that it doesn't have to be a belt that you grab; you can use anything to aid the throw such as the back of the attacker's jacket, trousers, jumper or shirt.

With the belt-assisted hip throw you simply reach, or better still throw, your right arm over the opponent's back and hook on to anything you can, as shown, turn your hip into the opponent and bend at the knees so that your bottom is pushing into his lower abdomen area. Straighten your legs, pulling the opponent on to your hips and throw him over and on to his back.

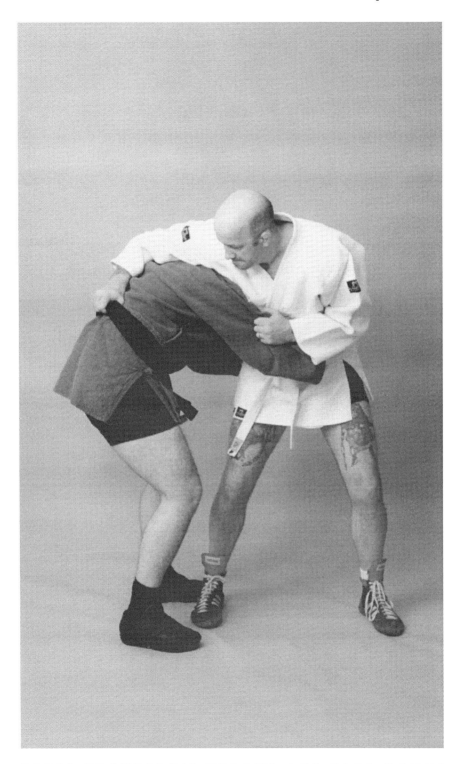

Sombo Russian Wrestling

Sombo Russian Wrestling

The Russians are very keen on this across-the-back type grip and make very good use of it in their free-fighting and self-defence.

Almost identical, other than the inclusion of the right leg used in a sweeping action, is the belt-assisted uchi mata.

This has exactly the same entry as the latter hip throw, only you should step a little deeper with the left leg and sweep the right leg high in between the opponent's legs, driving him on to his back.

Sombo Russian Wrestling

Belt-assisted Hip Throw

Again, a slight variation of the hip throw is the belt-assisted harai goshi. It uses the same entry, but step a little more to the right with your left leg and sweep the right leg to the outside of the opponent's right thigh, slamming him to the floor.

Sombo Russian Wrestling

Chapter 11
Belt-assisted Major Outside Reap

Another good belt-assisted throw is the devastating outside reap. I have been caught with this once or twice in randori so I can vouch for its potency.

With the major outside reap the catch is still the same throw your arm over the right shoulder of the opponent and grab his belt (or anything else). Step forward and to the outside of the opponent's right leg with your left leg, sweep your right leg hard and straight at the back of the opponent's right leg at the same time as you drive his bodyweight, via your right grip, on to the same leg. Slam him to the floor and on to his back.

Sombo Russian Wrestling

Conclusion

Of all the throws in the Russian system of sombo wrestling these detailed herein are the ones that I most favour. Of course there are a lot more, but many of those left are identical – or very similar – to those in other wrestling styles. I have tried not to repeat the same throws as those detailed in the other books in this series. To make these throws work you have to make them your own with persistent and accurate practise. It is not practise that makes perfect as people are always telling us; it is perfect practise that makes perfect. I once did thousands of outer reaping throws on a tree only to realise that I was doing it all wrong. This means starting all over again. Try to avoid this if you can. It'll save you many hours. Unlearning bad habits can be an arduous and very time-consuming task. When you do it wrong you become very good at a bad technique, then to get it right you have to take a backward step and relearn it right from the beginning. So take your time when you practise: quality is far better than quantity.

Sombo Russian Wrestling

As a final word I should reiterate that, as far as self-defence is concerned, I always believe that you should avoid a physical response whenever possible. Violence is not the answer in the majority of cases and a physical response should only be undertaken if no other option is open to you. I always try to avoid confrontational situations as much as possible; I employ verbal dissuasion if I can't escape, and loophole or posture if dissuasion has failed me. If and when the physical is called for I will attack the very first instant that I believe an opponent is going to attack me. Attack is the best means of defence.

If you make a mistake anywhere along the line and an opponent manages to grab hold of you, that is when the techniques in this book are going to come in handy. So throwing and grappling work only usually come into play when you have made a mistake.

For the record, I never court grappling range in a real-life scenario unless it is a one on one fight. Work from a fence if you have to be physical, attack using your hands and make the finish a clinical one.

However, as I have said we all make mistakes; even monkeys fall out of the trees. We should not be ignorant or naïve enough to believe that we are never going to make a mistake and hit the floor. Always prepare for the worst-case scenario, just in case.

Thank you very much for taking the time to read my book and good luck with your training.

God's blessing.

Geoff Thompson 2001

The Throws and Take-Downs of Judo

THE THROWS & TAKE-DOWNS OF

JUDO

GEOFF
THOMPSON

SUMMERSDALE

The Throws and Take-Downs of Greco-Roman Wrestling

THE THROWS & TAKE-DOWNS OF

GRECO-ROMAN WRESTLING

GEOFF THOMPSON

SUMMERSDALE

The Throws and Take-Downs of Freestyle Wrestling

THE THROWS & TAKE-DOWNS OF
FREESTYLE WRESTLING

GEOFF THOMPSON

SUMMERSDALE

Geoff Thompson's autobiography,
Watch My Back

GEOFF THOMPSON

WATCH MY BACK

'I train for the first shot
– it's all I need.'

'LENNIE MCLEAN HAD THE BRAWN, DAVE COURTNEY HAD THE
CHARM, BUT GEOFF THOMPSON IS IN A CLASS OF HIS OWN.' FHM

Anyone interested in Russian martial arts or Sombo please contact Mathew Clempner's FORMA UK at Federation of Russian Martial Arts. FORMA PO Box 45 Manchester M28 2JR

www.geoffthompson.com

www.summersdale.com